AMERICAN HEROES

Susan B. ANTHONY

By
Jane Corey

HOUGHTON MIFFLIN   BOSTON

Cover Background Image: Suffragists pose in front of the Capitol House Building, 1914.

Printed in China

ISBN-13: 978-0-618-67735-1
ISBN-10: 0-618-67735-6

5 6 7 8 9 10 - SDP - 12 11 10 09 08

Anthony's aunt, Hannah Anthony Hoxie, often spoke in the church Anthony went to as a girl. As Anthony listened to her aunt, she may have decided she could also speak about what she thought was right.

Speaking up wasn't easy for a young woman in the early 1800s. Many people thought women did not need an education. They thought women only needed to know how to do jobs such as cooking and washing.

In Anthony's home, girls learned the same things as boys. Anthony grew up expecting to become a strong, **independent** woman.

▶ Before washing machines, women scrubbed laundry by hand. Doing the laundry took a whole day.

CHAPTER 2

A Young Woman

To be an independent woman, Anthony needed a job. She was tall, with a strong voice, a straight back, and a sharp mind. What kind of work could she do? In the 1800s, teaching was one of the few jobs open to women, so Anthony became a teacher.

Anthony was paid much less than men who did the same work. "I am going to do something about it in my lifetime," she wrote in a letter to her father. When she complained, however, Anthony lost her job.

▶ Susan B. Anthony was a 28-year-old teacher when this picture was taken.

Anthony got a new job as the principal of the Girls' Department at Canajoharie (can uh juh HAIR ee) Academy in Canajoharie, New York. Her students worked hard. They did well on their tests.

After ten years of teaching there, Anthony wanted to do more. She wanted to work for **justice,** or fair treatment. She saw that many people in the United States were not being treated fairly.

In 1846, Anthony became head of the Girls' Department at Canajoharie Academy in New York.
▼

Academy

Teachers' House

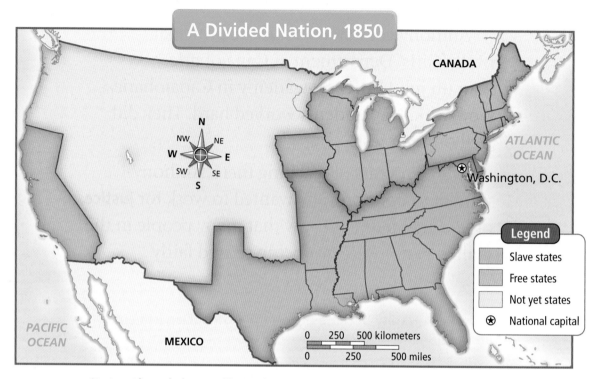

A Divided Nation, 1850

CANADA

ATLANTIC OCEAN

⊛ Washington, D.C.

Legend
- Slave states
- Free states
- Not yet states
- ⊛ National capital

PACIFIC OCEAN

MEXICO

0   250   500 kilometers

0   250   500 miles

▲ States that did not allow slavery were called free states.
States that allowed it were called slave states.

One injustice that angered Anthony was **slavery.**
Some states allowed slavery, but others did not.
Many people felt that slavery should not be
allowed anywhere.

The question of whether slavery should be
allowed divided people in the United States.
Feelings were strong on both sides of the issue.
People in the Anthony family were **abolitionists.**
They wanted to abolish, or get rid of, slavery.

Anthony quit her job and went to live with her parents in Rochester, New York. She wanted to spend all her time working against slavery. The Anthonys' house in Rochester was a meeting place for people who were fighting to end slavery.

Many abolitionists lived near Rochester. They helped enslaved African Americans who had escaped from slavery.

Anthony lived with her family in this red brick home in Rochester, New York.
▼

Frederick Douglass

▲ Frederick Douglass gave speeches at antislavery meetings and published an antislavery newspaper.

One of the most famous abolitionists in the United States, Frederick Douglass, lived in Rochester. Douglass had escaped from slavery. He often visited the Anthony house.

Douglass and many other abolitionists thought women should have the same rights as men. Anthony met many people in Rochester who shared her belief in equal rights.

CHAPTER 3

Justice for All!

In March 1851, something happened that changed Anthony's life. Her friend Amelia Bloomer introduced her to Elizabeth Cady Stanton. Stanton had organized a women's rights **convention** in Seneca Falls, New York, in 1848.

Anthony and Stanton liked each other right away. For the next 52 years, they worked together to win equal rights for women in the United States.

This memorial in Seneca Falls, New York, is called *When Anthony Met Stanton.*

▼

▲ Elizabeth Cady Stanton holds one of her children.

Anthony and Stanton made a good team. Each had something the other did not.

Stanton and her husband had seven children. She wanted to be home with her family, and she was a good writer. She stayed home and wrote speeches.

Anthony did not like to write, but she was a good **organizer** and speaker. She traveled to meetings and gave the speeches written by Stanton.

Anthony and Stanton wanted New York State to accept the right of married women to own property and businesses. They felt that changing the law was an important step toward equality.

Anthony traveled all over New York in the 1850s. She slept in cold hotel rooms and traveled through blizzards to give speeches.

All of Anthony's hard work helped. In 1860, the New York State **Legislature** passed a new law that allowed married women to own property.

▶ Anthony kept a careful record of all the money she spent on her trips.

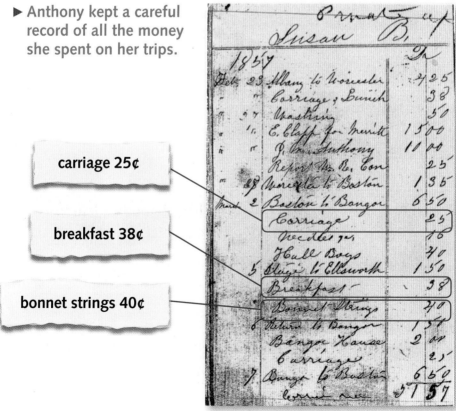

carriage 25¢

breakfast 38¢

bonnet strings 40¢

Anthony and Stanton wanted to win justice for all. That meant men and women, African Americans, and all other Americans.

In 1856, Anthony started to work for the Anti-Slavery Society in New York State. Both she and Stanton traveled and made speeches against slavery.

Stanton traveled to the World Anti-Slavery Convention in London in 1840, shown in this painting.
▼

Although many women worked to end slavery, they were not allowed to become the leaders of antislavery groups. Anthony and Stanton started a group for women who wanted to work against slavery. They called it the Women's National Loyal League. It was the first political group in the United States to be formed by women.

▶ This abolitionist button from the 1850s shows black and white hands joined together.

CHAPTER 4

The Right to Vote

In 1860, some slave states tried to leave the United States. The United States went to war to keep those states in the country. This was called the Civil War. After the war ended in 1865, slavery became illegal in the United States.

Anthony and abolitionists wanted to win the vote for freed slaves and women. In 1870, new laws recognized the right of freed African American men to vote.

Stanton and Anthony were the first to sign this petition to give freed slaves and women the right to vote.
▼

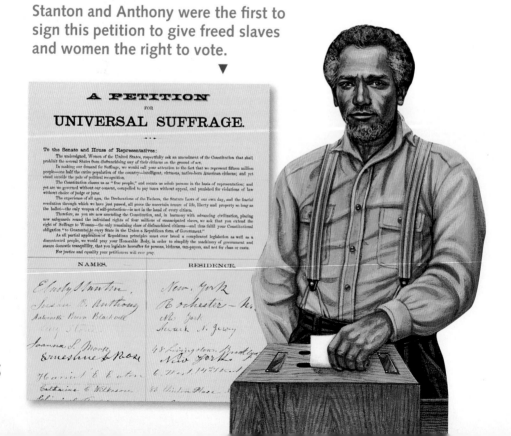

16

New laws that recognized the right of African American men to vote did not let women vote, however. Anthony thought that unless women could vote, they could never have equal rights under the law. To win the vote for women, Anthony and Stanton started a new group. It was called the National Woman **Suffrage** Association. Suffrage means the right to vote.

▲ People wore pins like these to show they thought women should be able to vote.

▲ Susan B. Anthony

▲ Elizabeth Cady Stanton

In 1872, Susan B. Anthony decided that although women were not allowed to vote, she was going to vote anyway. She believed that voting was her right. On November 1, she went to **register** to vote. After a short argument, she was allowed to sign up to vote in Rochester.

Four days later, on Election Day, Anthony voted for President of the United States. Nobody stopped her.

On November 18, Anthony was arrested. She was accused of voting illegally. Anthony was told that she would have a trial before a judge and jury. In the months before her trial, Anthony traveled around giving a speech called, "Is It a Crime for a Citizen of the United States to Vote?"

◀ Anthony wrote a letter to Stanton about voting. She said, "Well, I have been and gone and done it!"

▲ Anthony's trial was held at the United States Courthouse in Canandaigua, New York.

Anthony's trial took place in June 1873. The judge would not let her speak. Anthony's lawyer, however, did a very good job of convincing the jury that Anthony had not broken the law.

The judge was worried. If the jury said that Anthony had not broken a law, then all women in New York State would be allowed to vote. He told the jury that they had to say she had broken the law.

Anthony was told to pay a fine of $100. She said, "I shall never pay a dollar of your unjust penalty."

We know a lot about how women in the United States won the right to vote because Anthony and Stanton wrote a series of books. They knew that the struggle for suffrage was important. They knew that someday women would be able to vote. They wanted to leave an accurate record of what they had done to win suffrage. They called the books *The History of Woman Suffrage.* The first volume was published in 1881.

Anthony and Stanton worked together for women's rights for over 50 years.
▼

By the 1890s, Anthony had been working for years. Her **diligence** did not end, however.

In 1896, when she was in her seventies, Anthony traveled to California. She gave speeches along the way. In California she urged the legislature to recognize women's right to vote.

Younger women learned from her and traveled with her. They became new leaders in the struggle for voting rights for American women.

▶ Women beat drums, sang songs, marched, and gave speeches to win support for women's suffrage.

Anthony saw that people were changing their opinions. In the past, her ideas had angered some people. Now, people treated her like a hero.

By 1906, four states—Wyoming, Utah, Colorado, and Idaho—had allowed women to vote. Anthony urged other women to keep up the fight.

"Failure is impossible," she said.

Women from across the United States marched for women's suffrage in this 1912 parade in New York City.
▼

23

CHAPTER 5

Anthony's Legacy

In 1920, the law was changed to allow women in every state to vote. Anthony did not live to see that day, but her long years of work helped to make it happen.

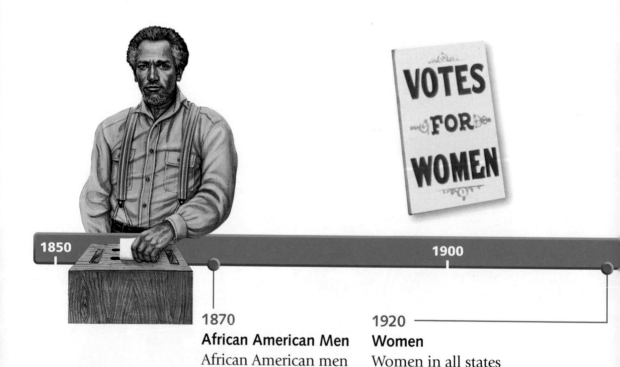

| 1850 | | 1900 | |

1870
African American Men
African American men are guaranteed suffrage.

1920
Women
Women in all states win suffrage.

Today, Susan B. Anthony is honored with the Susan B. Anthony dollar and with a plaque at the National Women's Hall of Fame, in Seneca Falls, New York.

The most important reminder of her work, however, takes place every time women in the United States vote, run for office, or serve in government. These are the rights for which Anthony fought. Using those rights is the best way to keep them.

1971
Young People
Voting age is lowered from 21 to 18 in every state.

1950　　　　　　　　　　　　　　　　　2000

1975
American Indians
Voting rights of American Indians are protected.

Activity Mapping the Life

Susan B. Anthony

Susan B. Anthony traveled all over the United States, giving speeches about women's suffrage. She convinced many people that women should have the same rights as men. Many states recognized the right of women to vote even before the law changed for the whole country.

1820: Adams, Massachusetts
Susan B. Anthony is born.

1872: Rochester, New York
Anthony votes for President and is arrested.

1890: Wyoming
Wyoming becomes the first state to recognize the right of women to vote.

Look at the map. Write a sentence to explain where women could vote before 1920.

WASHINGTON
1910

OREGON
1912

IDA
18

NEVADA
1914

CALIFORNIA
1911

PACIFIC
OCEAN

▶ This statue of Anthony is in Rochester, New York.

When and Where Women Could Vote

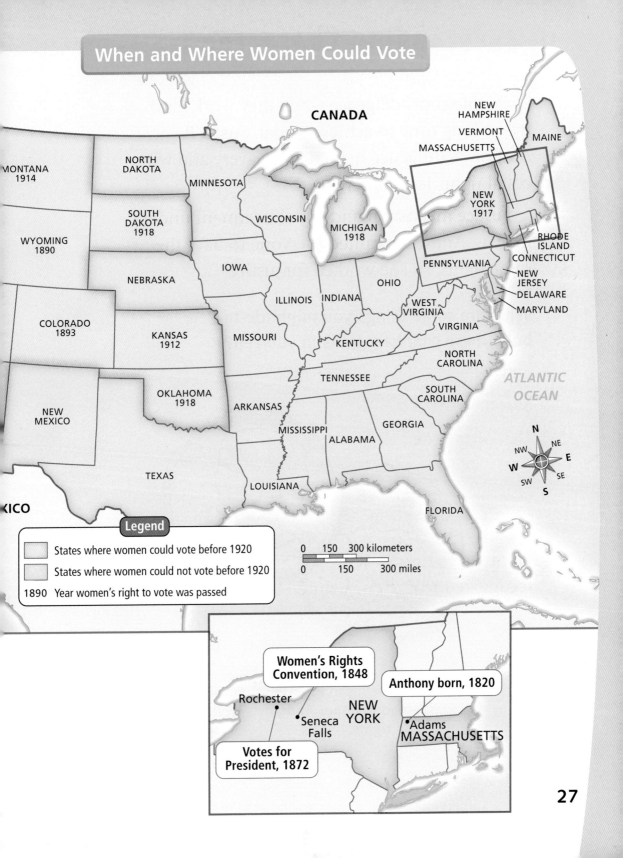

CANADA

NEW HAMPSHIRE
VERMONT
MASSACHUSETTS
MAINE

MONTANA
1914

NORTH DAKOTA

MINNESOTA

SOUTH DAKOTA
1918

WISCONSIN

MICHIGAN
1918

NEW YORK
1917

WYOMING
1890

IOWA

NEBRASKA

OHIO

PENNSYLVANIA

RHODE ISLAND
CONNECTICUT
NEW JERSEY
DELAWARE
MARYLAND

COLORADO
1893

KANSAS
1912

ILLINOIS

INDIANA

WEST VIRGINIA

VIRGINIA

MISSOURI

KENTUCKY

NORTH CAROLINA

NEW MEXICO

OKLAHOMA
1918

ARKANSAS

TENNESSEE

SOUTH CAROLINA

ATLANTIC OCEAN

TEXAS

MISSISSIPPI

ALABAMA

GEORGIA

LOUISIANA

FLORIDA

N
NW NE
W E
SW SE
S

MEXICO

Legend

States where women could vote before 1920

States where women could not vote before 1920

1890 Year women's right to vote was passed

0   150   300 kilometers
0   150   300 miles

Women's Rights Convention, 1848

Anthony born, 1820

Rochester

Seneca Falls

NEW YORK

Votes for President, 1872

Adams
MASSACHUSETTS

Understanding Character Traits

People show **diligence** when they work hard over a long time to achieve a goal. Susan B. Anthony's diligence helped end slavery and win equal rights for women.

Justice means fair and equal treatment under the law. Anthony wanted everyone to have the same rights, so she worked for justice.

What are some things you might do to build these character traits in yourself?

▲ In 1979, the Susan B. Anthony silver dollar was issued to honor Anthony's work for women's rights.

GLOSSARY

abolitionists people who want to end slavery (p. 8)

convention a formal meeting where people discuss a subject they are interested in (p. 11)

diligence working hard for a long time (p. 22)

independent being free to make one's own decisions (p. 5)

justice equal treatment under the law (p. 7)

legislature the law-making part of a government (p. 13)

organizer a person who gets others to work for a shared goal or cause (p. 12)

property something that is owned (p. 3)

Quaker a member of a religion that emphasizes equality among people (p. 4)

register to place one's name on an official list to do something (p. 18)

slavery a cruel system in which one person owns and controls another person (p. 8)

suffrage the right to vote (p. 17)

INDEX